LONDON MIDLAND
STEAM IN NORTH WALES

W. G. REAR

D. BRADFORD BARTON LIMITED

Frontispiece: Rebuilt 'Royal Scot' No.46156 *The South Wales Borderer* rounds the curve through Conway station under the town wall arch with a Holyhead – Euston express on 14 June 1962.   [A. Tyson]

© *copyright D. Bradford Barton 1979*   *2975/3W*   *ISBN 0 85153 225 X*

printed in Great Britain by Whitstable Litho Ltd., Whitstable, Kent
and bound by The Newdigate Press Ltd., Dorking for the publishers

D. BRADFORD BARTON LTD · Trethellan House · Truro · Cornwall · England

introduction

The London Midland lines in North Wales were well known to most enthusiasts, yet appear to have been neglected by photographers. Whilst compiling this volume, the author contacted many of the likely photographers, only to draw a blank, or obtain views in one of about four well known locations. As a result, it will be seen that the greater proportion of this book is the work of the author and Norman Kneale, and is concentrated on locations West of Llandudno.

The author worked for several years with British Railways, and became very friendly with the staff of Bangor shed. In the early 1950s, there was much activity, but even so, the first rumblings of closure were to be heard. Diesel units began to make their appearance, including the small A.C.V. three coach unit, which spent a couple of weeks growling up and down the Amlwch branch. The late J. M. Dunn made the forecast then that the days of Bangor shed were numbered. Despite this warning, and the belief that 'there was plenty of time left', many locations which would have provided good views remained unvisited. My own activities were concentrated on Caernarvon and the branches to Afonwen and Llanberis, whilst Norman worked around Bangor and on Anglesey.

A book of this nature takes time to prepare, and calls for much patience on the part of relatives. To this end, I would like to place on record my thanks to my family who 'put up with it', and state that without the encouragement of my wife Norma, this book would not have been completed. To photographers go grateful thanks, especially Norman Kneale. Lastly, I wish to place on record my thanks to all the footplate staff of Bangor shed, alas no more, especially Moi Edwards, Will Bach Bob Shunt, and to the memory of Trevor Williams, with his brother Bob 'Joy' Williams, who shared many happy hours with me. Also two members of Llandudno Junction shed, namely Tommy Gill and Bill Griffiths, who produced many fine runs along the coast which live on in memory.

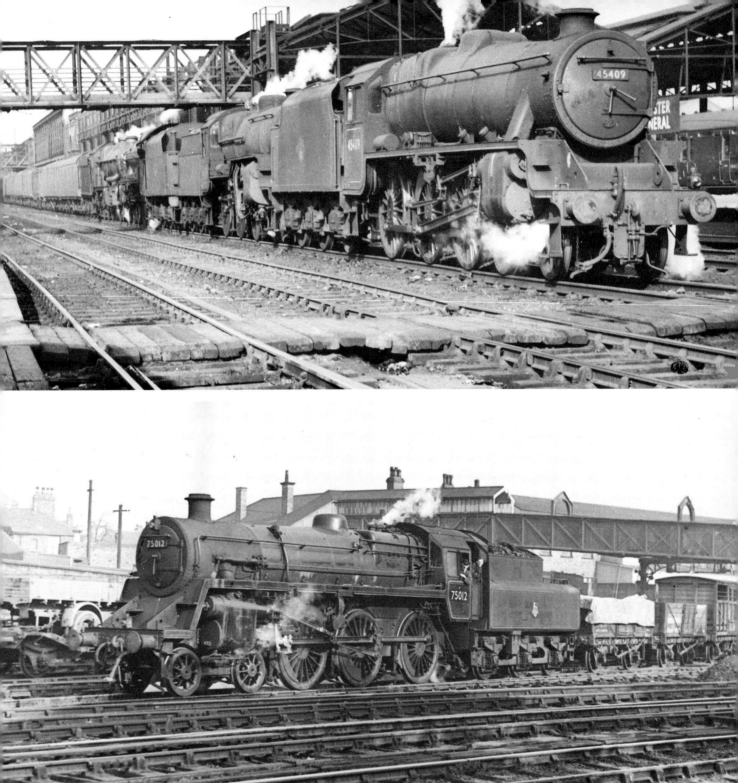

An afternoon Llandudno–Manchester train waits for the guard's right-away—and the 'peg' to come off—at Chester
(General) on 18 August 1963. No.46152 *The King's Dragoon Guardsman* in original form, is thought to have been the
member of the class renumbered as the No.6100 to go on tour in North America in 1933.   [W. L. Underhay]

ne of the first of the BR Standard Class 4 4-6-0s in the North Wales area was No.75012,
en here engaged on shunting duties in Chester goods yard in 1952. Drivers' comments
out the new locomotive were not very complimentary.   [W. G. Rear]

Class 5 No.45393 pulls out of Chester (General) with a North Wales train, and draws past No.44819—a scene typical of summer Saturdays at Chester until the demise of steam and the rationalisation of workings along the coast. The fine ex-LNWR signal gantry was for years a prominent feature at the west end of the station.
[Norman Kneale]

BR 'Britannia' Pacific No.70042 *Lord Roberts* draws out of Chester (General) and passes Number 4 signalbox with a train for Bangor on an evening in 1963. At this point the Birkenhead lines diverge to the right from the main North Wales coast line which is seen curving to the left.   [Norman Kneale]

A feature of working at Chester was the splitting of the main platform into two sections, thus enabling two trains to use the same face at once. This location was once the scene of a collision in the 1950s due to over-running of the signals. Here, 0-6-0T No.47266, on station shunting duties, adds a couple of parcels vans to the leading train, whilst Class 40 diesel-electric D218 waits at the Crewe end of the platform.

[Norman Kneale]

A general view of the west end of the station layout and Chester Number 6 box, showing the junction of the Birkenhead to North Wales lines which avoid using the General station and reversal of the motive power. A Standard Class 5 crosses from the down to the up line on the coast line, whilst a Class 40 waits its turn to cross onto the former GWR lines to Wrexham.

[Norman Kneale]

Class 5 No.45237 drifts into Chester cutting on the former GWR lines from Wrexham with a train of empty wagons, whilst Fairburn Class 4T No.42240 keeps pace on the ex-LMS coast lines. Two sets of running lines run parallel to Saltney Junction, about 1½ miles out of the city. There are two short tunnels on this section interspersed, as seen here, by vertical-sided deep cuttings in the sandstone.   [J. R. Carter]

Class 5 No.44892 in (ex-works) condition after a visit to Crewe, backs down towards Chester on the former GWR line, and is seen crossing the bridge over the Shropshire Union Canal locks, May 1961. [P. H. Hanson]

Class 2P 4-4-0 No.4067 gathers speed with a train to Rhyl, having just crossed the River Dee before entering the cutting near Saltney Junction. At the date of this photograph in May 1953, this locomotive was based at Rhyl shed and was being worked by Rhyl men.   [W. G. Rear]

Class 5 No.44917 heads a down freight for Mold Junction near Saltney Junction, having crossed the River Dee by the bridge, just visible beyond the road overbridge, September 1961.   [A. Tyson]

14

Two views of Holywell
Junction; above Stanier
2-6-0 No.42978 shunts
the station yard on the
up side, 28 April 1954.
Below, on the down
side, Ivatt 2-6-2T No.
41276 waits in the bay
platform with the
5.20 p.m. to Holywell
Town. This short
branch was worked
latterly by Rhyl shed,
using these Class 2
2-6-2 tanks, replacing
old ex-LNWR
'Coal Tanks'.

After they had been displaced by diesels from top link express passenger duties at Crewe, Camden and other main line sheds elsewhere on the Region, rebuilt 'Royal Scots' appeared much more frequently than formerly on the coast line. Here, No.46149 *The Middlesex Regiment* is waiting to leave Rhyl with a returning excursion to Birmingham on 3 June 1963.

[A. Tyson]

Standard Class 5 4-6-0 No.73014 passing Abergele on the slow line with a long rake of twenty coaches in June 1963. These are probably bound for one of the coastal resorts farther west to form two return excursions later in the day.

[A. Ty...]

No.45067, one of the first Vulcan Foundry-built batch of Class 5s turned out in 1934-35, gets away from Abergele with a Llandudno – Manchester (Exchange) train, June 1964. The section of line here skirts the shoreline, with holiday camps extending much of the way between Llandulas (west of Abergele) and Prestatyn, a distance of about ten miles.

[A. Tyson]

The four-track section ends at Llandulas, heading west, and a long cutting on a rising gradient of 1 in 100 takes the track into Penmaenrhos Tunnel (486 yards) under the limestone headland known as Penmaen Head, site of numerous large quarries. Compound No.41093, of Llandudno Junction shed (6G), leaving Penmaenrhos Tunnel on the approach to Old Colwyn, with an express for Llandudno.   [Rogers Jones]

Class 5 No.45300 heads into the sun with a Chester–Llandudno stopping train on an August afternoon in 1961, approaching Llandulas. The slow lines at each side were essential to accommodate the heavy flow of summer excursion traffic along the coast and in winter when the number of trains was very much reduced they were pressed into use as e.c.s. storage sidings—partly to relieve congestion elsewhere and partly to avoid the vandalism empty stock was subjected to in more populous areas in the North West.   [A. Tyson]

The Stanier-designed 'Black Fives' were the most common locomotive of all in post-war years on the North Wales main line. This is No.45067 waiting for the whistle at Colwyn Bay, 2 June 1963. Next stops are Llandudno Junction, Deganwy and then Llandudno.

[A. Tyson]

British Railways'
solitary Class 8 Pacific,
No.71000 *Duke of
Gloucester,* in Colwyn
Bay station with a
Holyhead train in 1961.
The 'Duke' made a few
appearances on the coast
line including this one.
    [Norman Kneale]

Rebuilt 'Jubilee'
No.45735 *Comet,* in the
up platform with a train
for Chester, 14 August
1953. [H. C. Casserley]

Compound No.41123, based at Llandudno Junction, passing Colwyn Bay gasworks with a train for Chester, in May 1953. After the constriction of double track only from Llandulas through Old Colwyn and along the restricted sea-front embankment to Colwyn Bay station, the main line again reverted to quadruple track beyond there, as far as Llandudno Junction.   [W. G. Rear]

An unidentified Class 5 approaching Colwyn Bay on the up slow line with an eight-coach Llandudno to Chester train in May 1953.   [W. G. Rear]

Class 5 No.45021 heads a Manchester train past all that remains of the former station of Mochdre and Pabo, between Colwyn Bay and Llandudno Junction. The signalbox here was retained for summer use, to split the long section and give additional line capacity. Close by here were the first water-troughs laid in Britain, in 1857; they were later moved to Aber, near Bangor. [Norman Kneale]

Llandudno Junction: a freight from Blaenau Ffestiniog behind Ivatt Class 2 No.41285, 28 August 1964.

[Derek Cross]

Caprotti valve-geared Class 5 No.44739 was based at Llandudno Junction shed, and was a regular on the Manchester 'Club' train. Here, it is seen coasting into Llandudno Junction with a summer Saturday extra for Llandudno. Below; 'Jubilee' No.45620 *North Borneo* coasts into 'the Junction' on the slow line with another special made up with assorted rolling stock. On the right, Class 2 No.41236 waits at the signals with a branch train from Blaenau Ffestiniog. [Rogers Jones]

For many years 4-4-0 compounds were a familiar sight on the coast run, and several were shedded at Llandudno Junction (when the shed code was '7A') and also at Holyhead. They spent the last of their days working semi-fast and local trips and here, 41166 leaves Llandudno Junction on the slow line towards Colwyn Bay with a semi-fast to Chester.
[Rogers Jones]

The shed at Llandudno Junction, showing the modern structure, alas now no more. The influx of British Railways Standard Class 2 tanks in the 84xxx series meant the transfer elsewhere of the Stanier and Ivatt 2-6-2Ts that had worked the Conway Valley line for many years. The view dates from 1963.

[Norman Kneale]

An unidentified 'Britannia' Pacific approaching Llandudno Junction a few days after entering service, working the down relief 'Day Mail'. This locomotive was one of the batch allocated to Holyhead shed (6J) specifically for working the 'Irish Mail' traffic. On this occasion, the train was routed through the station on the avoiding lines, as presumably the platform faces were occupied.   [Rogers Jones]

or some years Llandudno Junction was used as a store for locomotives, and it was a common sight to see long line of engines out of service 'parked' on the original line from the Conway Valley (which was verted when the station was rebuilt before the turn of the century). The group shown here, taken on 2 July 1960, includes Nos.40095, 40130, 40535, 41236, 40133, 43378, 47394, 40008, 40048 and 0058.
                                                                                                                                [A. Tyson]   29

One of the innovations designed to attract passengers to the railways in the 1950s was the special shuttle service worked along the coastal resorts between Rhyl and Llandudno. The standard formation was composed of an Ivatt 2-6-2T, based at Rhyl (6K) shed, with three suburban coaches and worked as a push & pull unit. It had the added distinction of being named *The Welsh Dragon,* and was complete with roof boards on the carriages plus a headboard for the locomotive. The headlamp brackets held the board, as can be seen in the photograph. This scene shows No.41224 working past the level crossing at Llandudno Junction on the trip to Rhyl.   [Rogers Jones

Rebuilt 'Patriot' No.45523 *Bangor* with a Llandudno – Euston train eases round the sharp curve from beside the Conway estuary and Deganwy to join the main coast line into Llandudno Junction station; August 1960. In high summer this was a very busy section of line.

[Derek Cross]

A Holyhead to Llandudno train in Deganwy station, with 2-6-2T No.40083 at its head. The Stanier tank has brought the train from Llandudno Junction, as a reversal was involved there; 14 June 1962.   [A. Tyson]

32

ubilee' No.45599 *Bechuanaland* on a return excursion, made up largely of ex-LNER Gresley stock, aiting to leave Llandudno in August 1962. The 1950s and early 1960s saw some interesting workings in e high summer season. Regular workings of ex-LNER locomotives from Eastern Region to Llandudno ok place, including B1s. [A. Tyson]

Class 5 No.44680 approaches Llandudno Junction shortly after emerging from the Conway Tubular bridge. The line on the left of the photograph leads down to a small jetty, but is usually used for the storage of stock. [Rogers Jones]

A view from the leading compartments on a down train of the approach to Conway Tubular bridge. Below; the same scene photographed from the seaward side of another down train. 1961. [A. Tyson]

'Jubilee' No.45556 *Nova Scotia* passing under the walls of Conway Castle before entering the twin tube of the bridge across the river. It is believed that this photograph was the 3.50 p.m. Bangor to Chester with the author on the footplate—but actually taking a breather before resuming duties for the remainder of the trip . . . [Rogers Jones]

Overleaf: An up parcels train from Holyhead eases round the sharp curve through Conway station and the walls of the castle en route for Crewe, 28 August 1964.

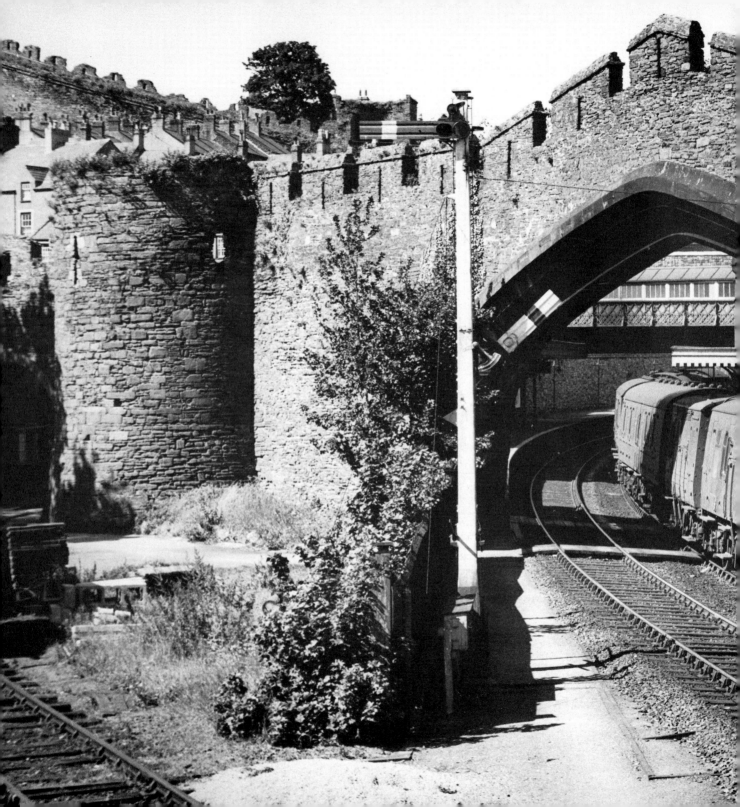

Another view of Conway station. Here, Bangor shed's Class 5 No.45144 pulls into the station with a stopping train to Llandudno Junction, from Holyhead, on 14 June 1962.
[A. Tyson]

2-6-4T No.42425 with a five coach 'all-stations' from Chester to Bangor, near Penmaen-mawr in August 1960.
[Derek Cross]

Rebuilt 'Royal Scot' No.46135 *The East Lancashire Regiment,* working the "Horse & Carriage" from Holyhead to London, skirting the sea front just east of Penmaenmawr, on 10 August 1960. This parcels train was always made up to phenomenal loads with the heavy Irish parcel, secondary mail and other traffic.
[Derek Cross]

The fireman's view of Aber troughs, taken from the footplate of a Llandudno Junction to Bangor train.

[Norman Kneale.

Rebuilt 'Royal Scot' Class 4-6-0 No.46155 *The Lancer* leaving Llandegai Tunnel near Bangor with an express from Holyhead to Chester in the early 1960s.　　[Norman Kneale]

Class 5 No.44804, of 16C shed, emerging from Llandegai Tunnel with a Saturday extra on 20 May 1967.

Another Class 5, this time No.45282, from Llandudno Junction shed, passing Tai Meibion, between Bangor and Aber, in the mid-1960s. Many of the regular workings had unofficial titles, this one being known as the up "Holyhead Meat" and usually consisting of insulated containers or vans.   [Norman Kneale

Fairburn 2-6-4T No.42236 of Chester shed pulls away from Bangor station with a Caernarvon to Chester train.

A view from the footplate of a Class 5, working light engine from Llandudno Junction to Holyhead, taken as the locomotive emerges from the tunnel, at the eastern (or Chester) end of Bangor station. The signal indicates a clear path through the down centre line.

[Norman Kneale]

Stanier Pacific No.46237 *City of Bristol* disappears into Belmont Tunnel after calling at Bangor with a Holyhead train in the final year of the classes brief appearance on the Welsh coast.

A general view of Bangor motive depot in the early 1960s. Some dmus are in evidence, being parked on th[e] down side platform face. Alongside them, carriages are stored, with the shed itself dividing the carriag[e] park. This view was taken early in the morning, with locomotives being prepared for work.

[Norman Kneale]

When conversation turns to railways around Bangor, and in particular in the period 1950-55, two 'personalities' are involved, both shown here. The first is Ivatt's 2-6-2T No.41200, which spent the greater part of its working life at the shed, whilst the second 'character' was the late J. M. Dunn, for many years shed master at Bangor. This view was taken in 1952. [W. G. Rear]

Class 2T No.41204, one of Bangor's own Ivatt 2-6-2 tanks, pulls away from the down platform during the course of shunting duties at the station on an afternoon in June 1963.

Bangor shed, like many others, was inclined to become congested, particularly as it had the misfortune to be sited between two hills which restricted space even more. Entry to the station was through a tunnel. All the goods yard traffic, together with access to motive power, carriage and permanent way sidings, were located at the western or Holyhead end. Some idea of the complex layout may be gained from this view, which also shows on shed 'Jubilee' No.45661 *Vernon* with Norman Kneale in the driver's seat. Alongside is Ivatt 2-6-2T No.41234.

Class 5 No.45345 outside Bangor shed.

With safety valves lifting, Class 5 No.44865 stands at the down platform at Bangor. Pacific No.46225 *Duchess of Gloucester,* in immaculate condition, is coasting into the up platform with a Holyhead to Chester express. *Below:* No.46225 *Duchess of Gloucester,* again with a lightweight train of five coaches, easing past Bangor No.2 signalbox, negotiating the pointwork leading to the up platform, with a Holyhead to Crewe train. [Norman Kneale]

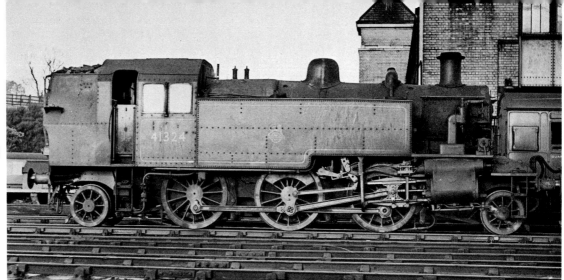

For a while, Ivatt Class 2T No.41324 was allocated to Bangor shed, and is seen here on the station shunt in 1953 shortly before it was transferred out of the district.

[W. G. Rear]

4-6-0 No.45249 drawing out of the down side relief road at Bangor with a train of parcels vans. [Norman Kneale]

Stanier Class 5 No.45282 held by signals on the centre road at Bangor with a train for Holyhead, May 1962.

[Norman Kneale]

British Railways Standard Class 4 2-6-4T No.80102 pilots Class 5 No.45275 as they emerge from Belmont Tunnel with the 10.43 a.m. from Portmadoc to Manchester (Saturdays only) in the summer of 1962. The chalked numerals on the bunker indicate the working, and the small figures chalked by the driver's door— '7.18' & 'Sat', were for the guidance of the crew allocated to this working. The 2-6-4T will be detached at the station platform leaving the Class 5 to continue alone.

[Norman Kneale]

Fairburn 2-6-4T No.42258 'on shed' at Bangor between turns. Six of this class, together with three of the heavier Stanier locomotives, were residents of 6H for many years. Shortly after this photograph was taken, this locomotive, plus three others, were exchanged with Scottish Region for four of the Fowler version. [W. G. Rear]

For a while, this push-and-pull two-coach unit, powered by Standard Class 2 No.84003, worked alongside dmus on the Amlwch branch and is seen here leaving Menai Bridge on the outward journey in March 1964.
[Norman Kneale]

Britannia' Pacific No.70027 draws away from Bangor tation with a down Holyhead train. [Norman Kneale]

4-6-0 Class 5 No.45050 pulling out of the goods yard at Menai Bridge with a mixed freight.

[Norman Kneale]

A rare visitor to the Chester & Holyhead line was BR Standard Pacific No.70000 *Britannia* herself, seen here passing through Menai Bridge with a Holyhead to Crewe fitted freight. [Norman Kneale]

Class 5 No.44775 rounds the curve approaching Menai Bridge with yet another fitted freight for Crewe from Holyhead. The lines on the left are the branch for Caernarvon and beyond.

[Norman Kneale]

Class 5 No.45091 leans to the curve as it emerges from the Britannia Tubular Bridge with a Holyhead to Chester train in 1961.   [Norman Kneale]

A view approaching the Britannia Bridge from the Anglesey side, on the British Railways Television Train, 24 September 1961, on the occasion of an excursion from Manchester to Llanfair P.G. 2-6-4T No.42209 can just be seen on the curve, running bunker-first.

[A. Tyson]

Summer Saturdays saw series of light engines and empty stock workings between Bangor and Penychain, near Pwllheli, over the Afonwen line. Here, two Class 2 2-6-0s return to Bangor after working the 9.08 a.m. Manchester to Portmadoc trip (from Bangor), and are seen coasting down Treborth bank into Menai Bridge. [Norman Kneale]

Fowler Class 4F No.44389, based at Llandudno Junction shed, emerges from the Britannia Bridge with a train of empty mineral wagons. Repairs to the bridge necessitated wrong line working on the occasion. This scene is taken from the Caernarvon side.
[Norman Kneale]

Menai Bridge was always the scene of much activity, 24 hours a day, with the exception of Sundays, until 1964, when strangulation of the local branch lines commenced. Here, Class 4T No.42212 stands at the up platform with a train from Caernarvon to Bangor, whilst No.41234, an Ivatt 2-6-2T, pauses on the Holyhead line, before returning to shunting duties in the goods yard.
[Norman Kneale]

British Railways Standard Class 4 No.75035 rolls down the bank from Treborth into Menai Bridge station with a train from Caernarvon to Chester.
[Norman Kneale]

Ivatt 2-6-2T No.41234
at Gaerwen station with
the 1.05 p.m. to
Amlwch, 23 August
1961.   [A. Tyson]   67

A goods train from Holyhead to Menai Bridge trundles slowly through Bodorgan station
in 1964.
[Norman Kneale]

Station name boards: less well known than the almost internationally famous Llanfair P.G. was Amlwch. When photographed in 1961, its rope letters were painted red against a smartly painted brick panel background.

At Amlwch, terminus of the branch from Gaerwen, No.84003 fills its tanks, prior to returning to the station platform for the run to Bangor. This view was taken in July 1964.
[Norman Kneale]

The up 'Irish Mail', with fourteen on, making up lost time as a result of a late start sweeps past Gaerwen No.2 signalbox en route from Holyhead. 'Britannia' Pacifics were the successors on this top-link Holyhead turn to 'Royal Scots' and 'Claughtons'.
[Rev. A. C. Cawston]

The climb out of Holyhead station is steep, and with locomotives just 'off shed' with a 'green fire' meant that smoke effects were common—much to the satisfaction of photographers. Here, 'Britannia' No.70024 *Vulcan,* formerly of the Western Region but at the time of the photograph based at Crewe North, pulls away with a heavy train for Crewe.

[Norman Kneale]

On the line from Menai Bridge to Caernarvon and Afonwen, the first summit is reached beyond Treborth. The line falls away steeply, and burrows under a hill through twin tunnels, which are of very close bore. To avoid the possibility of a blow-back the practice was to keep steam 'on' until the tunnels were cleared. Here 2-6-4T No.42157 bursts out with an Afonwen train on 4 October 1952.   [W. G. Rear]

Between Treborth and Port Dinorwic on the Afonwen line, was the signalbox at Port Siding, which controlled access to the dock at Port Dinorwic. Here, a Stanier 2-6-4T on a Caernarvon-Menai Bridge goods picks up some wagons, whilst ex-L & Y 0-6-0 No.52407 keeps out of the way, before resuming shunting duties on the quayside.   [W. G. Rear]

Port Dinorwic station is a building of imposing structure, located on the up side platform, and contrasts greatly with the humble shelter on the down line, which resembles an open-sided cattle shed. The main building was something of a white elephant, as traffic never justified its erection. For a short period in Bangor shed's history, a batch of standard BR Class 4 2-6-4 tanks replaced the LMS-designed ones. The newer locomotives were popular with the crews, but were transferred away again after a very short stay. Here, No.80094 works a Bangor–Afonwen local in 1957.

The 1950s saw additional traffic come to the Afonwen and other lines, with the introduction of the 'Land Cruise' excursion trains. At the peak of their popularity, there were four of these a day at times. These are two views of 'Land Cruise' trains passing through Caernarvon. *Above:* Ivatt 2-6-0 No.46435 pulls out of the station and passes No.1 signalbox with the Llandudno–Rhyl–Corwen–Barmouth–Caernarvon–Llandudno train, identified by the reporting number 662. *Below:* on three or four very rare occasions, until BR Standard Class locomotives could be drafted into the area to cover this working, ex-GWR locomotives were used to provide motive power for the 'cruise' which started at Criccieth, and worked in the reverse direction. In this working, the locomotive and crew were supplied by Pwllheli shed.

[W. G. Rear]

Fairburn 2-6-4T No.42283 pauses for the signal prior to working a Caernarvon – Menai Bridge goods in January 1965. The locomotive had not long returned from overhaul at Cowlairs works, hence the pristine condition of the paintwork. It is standing on the release road from the coal yard at the Bangor end of Caernarvon station. [Norman Kneale]

Fairburn 2-6-4T No.42156, still sporting the early British Railways lettering on its tanks, runs into Caernarvon station past No.1 signalbox, on a Saturday afternoon in June 1952, with a Bangor to Pwllheli local. The photograph was taken from the site of the former locomotive shed, demolished in the late 1930s. [W. G. Rear]

2-6-4T No.42489 departing from Caernarvon with a Pwllheli – Bangor train, 17 May 1962.

Stanier 2-6-2T No.40132 coasts down the bank near Caernarvon harbour with 'The Welshman' from Portmadoc and Pwllheli to Euston, in May 1952. Despite the appearance of double track, this is in fact two single lines, the nearer metals being the branch from Caernarvon to Llanberis. [W. G. Rear]

Ivatt 2-6-0 No.43052 pauses to take water by Caernarvon No.2 signalbox, prior to working Stanier Pacific No.6203 *Princess Margaret Rose* forward to its resting place at Butlin's holiday camp at Penychain, near Pwllheli, in September 1962. [Norman Kneale]

A quarter of a mile from the location of the upper photograph, the two lines had parted company. Here Stanier Class 4T No.42588 of Bangor shed climbs the bank towards Dinas, formerly the junction with the Welsh Highland Railway, in July 1952, whilst working a Bangor–Pwllheli local.

[W. G. Rear]

Principal station between Caernarvon and Afonwen was Penygroes, which, in addition to being a staff changing point, was a junction for the short branch to Nantlle, closed to passenger traffic in 1932. Here, Stanier 2-6-4T No.42585 draws out of the station with a Bangor to Afonwen local in August 1961. [J. Edgington]

Fairburn 2-6-4T No.42258, working bunker first, pulls into the loop at Dinas, with an Afonwen to Bangor local, one wet September afternoon in 1952. [W. G. Rear]

The climb out of Penygroes station towards Afonwen was for over a mile at a gradient of 1 in 49, and resulted in the need for assistance for most trains on summer Saturdays. In this photograph, two 2-6-4 tanks (Nos.42156 and 42628) on a Butlin's special make short work of the climb—seen snaking away in the background—on 11 July 1953. [W. G. Rear]

Stanier 2-6-4T No.42460 waits on the Nantlle branch at Penygroes with the Nantlle to Menai Bridge goods, one wet March morning in 1952—a view taken from the footplate of an Afonwen bound train. [W. G. Rear]

83

The summit of the Afonwen line was between Penygroes and Pant Glas, and then steam was shut off, apart from pulling away from the stations. The fireman's work was now more relaxed, and the journey to Afonwen was usually spent 'on the seat', after cleaning the footplate. In this scene is W 524, one of the procession of Saturday special extra trains for Butlin's holiday camp near Pwllheli. Albert Victor Williams, of No. 1 link at Bangor, in charge of 2-6-4T No.42157, is enjoying the view as he approaches Pant Glas station, as are the crew of No.40102, on 8 August 1953.   [W. G. Rear]

Fairburn 2-6-4T No.42157, of Bangor shed, ambles down the bank and along the harbour with the Llanberis to Caernarvon goods, before climbing the stiff 1 in 49 up to the station and goods yard at Caernarvon, in June 1952. [W. G. Rear]

For various reasons, the Ivatt 2-6-2Ts did not work many passenger turns over the Afonwen line, although they were quite capable of covering most of the workings during the winter, when loadings were lighter. Nevertheless they were scheduled to work some turns on summer Saturday afternoons, and here No.41223 of Bangor shed is seen drawing away from Afonwen station with the 7.05 p.m. to Bangor on 19 June 1954.
[W. G. Rear]

Stanier 2-6-4T No.42444, based for the summer season at Bangor shed, leans over to take the very sharp curve near Seiont brickworks siding on the outskirts of Caernarvon, on the Llanberis branch, in August 1953. *Below:* No.42617 returns with an articulated two-coach unit to Caernarvon, near the site of Pontrug station, in June 1953.   [W. G. Rear]

The intermediate stations on the Llanberis branch were extremely short, being only able to accommodate three coaches without drawing up more than once. Here, British Railways Stoneland Class 4 No.75009 waits at Cwm y Glo station with a demolition train prior to the return trip to Caernarvon.
[Norman Kneale]

The last scheduled goods train to Llanberis, prior to complete closure of the line, in the charge of 2-6-4T No.42489, shown here at Pontrhythallt station in October 1964.

This is the very last standard gauge train to use Llanberis station; Class 5 No.44711, of Llandudno Junction shed, waits by the platform before returning to Caernarvon with empty wagons.　　　　　[Norman Kneale]

Stanier 2-6-4T No.42617 skirts Llyn Padarn with a return afternoon excursion
from Llanberis to Rhyl and Prestatyn in September 1952.   [W. G. Rear]

Driver M. Edwards, of Bangor shed, brings 2-6-4T No.42460 into Llanberis station with empty stock, for a Saturday excursion to Manchester for the district's annual Sunday schools trip, 3 October 1953.

[W. G. Rear]

A regular in later steam days on the Blaenau Ffestiniog branch (from Llandudno Junction) was Ivatt 2-6-2T No.41236, seen here drawing into Bettws-y-Coed station with the 12.25 p.m. Llandudno Junction – Blaenau Ffestiniog, in August 1953.

[W. G. Rear]

Ivatt 2-6-2T No.41236, of Llandudno Junction shed, with a three coach Blaenau Ffestiniog train in the Conway valley. This extremely scenic branch is still open and deservedly popular among summer visitors as well as helping meet the transport needs of this rural area of North Wales.

[Rogers Jones]

Before the Ivatt 2-6-2Ts took over the working of the Conway Valley line, the Stanier version of the same wheel arrangement performed the task for many years. Here, No.40083 stands at the head of a Llandudno train in Blaenau Ffestiniog station, dwarfed by the vast slate tips; July 1951. [W. G. Rear]

In LNWR and LMSR days, the stalwarts on the Blaenau branch, particularly for freight traffic—once quite heavy—were the Webb 0-6-0 Crewe-built "Cauliflowers". These were time expired by the early 1950s and No.58365 had only a short period of service left before her when photographed at the branch terminus on 12 October 1951.

[D. H. Ballantyne]

Towards the end of steam operations on the Conway Valley line to Blaenau Ffestiniog, the latter station was rebuilt, and its layout simplified. The line was extended to connect up with the former GWR branch from Bala Junction, although the latter was terminated beyond Trawsfynydd, providing a rail link for the atomic power station. This line can be seen leading away to the left of the photograph. Freight working at the date of this photograph (1964) was still by steam, and here Class 5 No.44711 awaits departure time in the station yard.

[Norman Kneale]